W9-AKN-158

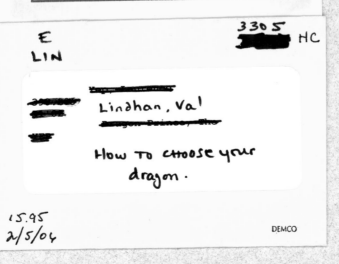

How to Choose Your Dragon

RON and VAL LINDAHN

LONGSTREET PRESS, INC.
Atlanta, Georgia

To Faye and Tom Daniels and Pat and Scott Lindahn for encouraging our imaginations.
To Barbara and Brad Strickland for keeping us in touch with the real world.
— Val Lindahn, July 1996

◆

For the children in my life who have given me an excuse to let my imagination play: Sheila, Kaitlyn, Kelly, Stacey, David, Kara, and especially Sean. Melissa, Jeffery, and Ashley — thanks for modeling. And for the beautiful Princess Valena, who got to know the dragons, made copious notes so I could learn about them too, and painted the wonderful pictures that brought them to life for me — thanks for letting me help with your book.
— Ron Lindahn, July 1996

Published by
LONGSTREET PRESS, INC.
A subsidiary of Cox Newspapers,
A subsidiary of Cox Enterprises, Inc.
2140 Newmarket Parkway, Suite 118
Marietta, GA 30067

Printed in the United States of America

1st printing 1996

Library of Congress Catalog Card Number: 96-76502

ISBN: 1-56352-325-6

Book and jacket design by Jill Dible

The Dragon

A Dragon can be a wonderful pet.
There are things you should know
if you haven't one yet.

With all their colors and shapes and sizes,
young Dragons are cute
and filled with surprises.

Hatched from an egg like an everyday bird,
they chirp when first born —
well, that's what I've heard.

Playful and smart, or quiet and shy,
some crawl on their bellies
while others can fly.

Some breathe fire and others perfume
with a scent that's like flowers
filling the room.

I wouldn't trade the time that I spend
with my wonderful Dragon,
my very best friend.

From *Old Missus Milliwhistle's Book of Beneficial Beasties*

Preface

One fine autumn day a pretty amazing thing happened in the sleepy little town of Clayton. A delivery truck pulled right up in front of Uncle Fred's Pet Shop. The driver unloaded several boxes marked "Fragile" and "Do Not Drop" and "This Side Up." He stacked the boxes just inside the front door and drove away whistling softly to himself.

Uncle Fred opened the first box. It was filled with squishy little white beads. He reached his hand down into the beads and touched something roundish and hard and warm. Then Uncle Fred pulled out a large blue-and-red-spotted egg. In all his years in the pet shop business he had never seen anything like it. He reached back into the box and found two more eggs.

Ten minutes later the floor was littered with empty boxes. All the colors of the rainbow glistened on the pile of eggs sitting on the table before him. "What could they be?" he asked himself.

Just then Melissa arrived. Melissa loved animals. She liked to visit Uncle Fred's Pet Shop on her way home from school.

Uncle Fred called Melissa over, pointing to the table with its pile of mysterious eggs.

"What do you make of these?" he said.

As Melissa and Uncle Fred watched, one of the eggs started to move. It rocked. It rolled, just a bit. It shook, then it started to split.

Melissa looked at Uncle Fred, her mouth open in surprise. Uncle Fred looked at Melissa, eyebrows raised in astonishment.

One after another, the rest of the eggs on the table began to quiver and quake. As Melissa and Uncle Fred looked on in wonder and amazement, a gold-colored egg, right up front, cracked wide open.

"What's that?" exclaimed Melissa.

Uncle Fred shrugged, "Don't know. It looks something like a lizard, and a little like a bird."

"It's so cute!" Melissa said almost whispering.

"If I didn't know better I'd say it could be a dinosaur." Uncle Fred remarked in a thoughtful manner.

Just then the little, green, bug-eyed creature tottering on the table before them sneezed, and a tendril of smoke curled up from one nostril above its beak. It sneezed again with so much force it toppled over backwards, landing on its behind.

"It's a baby dragon!" Melissa exclaimed in wide-eyed wonder.

Uncle Fred scratched his head, thought for a moment, and finally said, "I can't for the life of me think of what else it could be."

Then, one after another, the eggs on the table cracked open. Awestruck, Melissa and Uncle Fred watched as a dozen baby dragons emerged and began moving among the pieces of broken shell littering the table. And they were all different!

Some had wings, while others didn't. A few were striped or spotted. They were long and slender, short and stocky, with pointed snouts and flattened faces. It was almost more than Uncle Fred and Melissa could take in all at once.

"Can I have one?" Melissa implored after a moment of stunned silence.

Uncle Fred scratched his head again, thinking hard. Finally he said, "If it's all right with your mom and dad, you can take them all home. I'll hire you to take care of them and find out as much as you can about them. I can't do it here, don't have the space. Before I sell a pet I have to know something about it. What it likes and what it doesn't like, if it's easy to train or difficult. Just like each breed of dog has its own special traits, I'm sure these little rascals will be as different as day and night. Are you interested?"

Melissa looked at Uncle Fred with eyes as big as saucers.

"You really mean it?" she stammered. "All of them?"

"If you're up to the challenge . . . and your mom and dad agree," he said with a smile.

"You bet I am," she beamed. "I can't wait to tell my brother Jeffery."

"Well then, let's call your folks," Uncle Fred said, reaching for the phone.

Melissa's parents agreed to let her bring the dragons home under two conditions. First, that she keep up with her homework and maintain her good grades. And second, that she be completely responsible for their care and feeding. Melissa made solemn promises to both conditions, and she kept them very well.

As part of her assignment Uncle Fred asked Melissa to keep a detailed notebook. She was to describe everything she learned about keeping dragons as pets. Melissa's notebook contains her observations and much that she learned from books in the library. You will find it most useful if you choose to have a dragon as a pet.

How to Choose Your Dragon

How to Choose Your Dragon

Many people think dragons exist only in fairy tales. They believe the stories that tell of dragons as giant fire-breathing monsters who terrorize the countryside. Because of these stories dragons are misunderstood. They have a hard time making friends and finding good homes because people are afraid of them.

The truth is that dragons make wonderful pets. They love being with people. They are easy to care for and make loyal, friendly companions. Dragons are fascinating to be around, and some can even be trained to help out around the house.

Dragons come in many sizes. Some are as small as a hamster, but most are the size of cats and dogs. They also come in many different shapes and colors.

Just like different kinds of dogs have their own individual traits, each kind of dragon has its own special personality. A few are quiet and shy, but most love to be around people and like to get right in the middle of things. There are also some dragons who just naturally get into mischief, but most are very well behaved.

The worst mischief-makers are Camos. They are always hungry, and they eat almost anything. They constantly beg for snacks, and if you're not careful, they will sneak the food right off your plate when you're not looking.

Camos are very smart. It doesn't take long for them to learn where all of the food in the house is kept. If you decide to adopt a Camo, it is best to get dragon-proof locks for your kitchen cabinets and refrigerator — and don't forget the cookie jar.

Once I made the mistake of letting the Camos see me throw food scraps in the garbage can. Tang and Booger ran around the can wailing like sirens until I lured them away with cookies and milk.

The name 'Camo' is short for camouflage, and Camos are related to chameleons. Instead of turning the color of their environment, Camos often turn the color of something they want to eat.

You must watch your other pets around Camos. They won't actually eat your other pets, but they think it's great fun to tease them. They especially like to get fish excited by sticking their heads in the tank, or tapping on the glass with their noses.

Camos will also sneak up very quietly behind birds in a cage. All at once they will make loud cat sounds. While the poor birds squawk and flutter their wings in fright, the Camos look at each other in innocent surprise—as if they didn't know what all the fuss was about. Sometimes Camos are not very nice.

If you are patient, you can teach Camos many tricks. When they are not looking for food or taking a nap, they can be trained to help put your toys back in your toy chest.

Most dragons will eat the same food you eat. You must be careful to see that they get a balanced diet. They need lots of fruits and vegetables to stay healthy. They like table scraps, and are especially fond of desserts. Too many sweets are not good for them. They can have one or two cookies, or a small piece of chocolate cake, but no more, or else they'll get too nervous and fidgety.

Dragons like a nice soft place to sleep, like on top of clothing that they find lying on the floor. If you don't make a special place for them to sleep, they will make a nest of socks and t-shirts under your bed. If you can't find your socks, look under the bed. You may have a dragon in the house.

Dragons keep themselves very clean. As long as they are healthy and well cared for, they smell quite pleasant. Each kind of dragon has its own special scent. Camos smell a bit like cinnamon, Dweebs smell like butterscotch, and Thumpers smell like chocolate.

Dragons do not normally need to take a bath unless they have been playing outside in the dirt. But they love water and may surprise you by jumping right in the bathtub with you when you are taking your bath.

When you wash your dragon, use warm water, but not too hot because dragons are very sensitive to temperature. For a special treat you can give them a bubble bath. Bubbles tickle their noses and make them giggle. Dragons tend to get very playful in the water and like lots of toys. Have plenty of towels handy because they splash quite a bit and may get water all over the floor.

You must be careful with your dragon if you have cats or dogs in the house. Most dragons will get along very well with your other pets, but it may take some time for them to get used to each other. It will help if you play with them together so they know it is all right to be friends.

If you have a Nidget dragon, you must take special care. Nidgets are one of the smallest breeds of dragon, and they are very timid and shy and easily frightened. When they feel threatened, they will hide and shiver for hours.

Once after being startled by a cat, our Nidget, Squeaky, hid in the cookie jar, and I didn't find her until after supper. Every time the front door slams, she crawls inside the slot of the video tape player to hide.

If your Nidget should become badly frightened, you can calm it down by taking it for a walk outside. If you smile and tell it a nice story, it will cheer up and be happy again.

Squeaky loves anything that is round. Whenever she finds marbles or grapes lying around, she hides them in one of my socks. Once she spent a whole day sitting on my brother's baseball. I guess she thought it was an egg.

Most dragons are very playful and love to play games with children best of all. The Dweebs are especially funny when they play. Once Aunt Edna found my cousin Ashley dressing Sparky in one of my doll's outfits. The shoes wouldn't fit because Dweebs have very big feet.

When Sparky was all dressed up, he started to slide his feet from side to side like he was dancing, and all the while he cooed and chirped. He was so happy. After that Sparky would bring dresses out and put them in Ashley's lap when he wanted to play dress-up.

Dweebs are color-blind and have a terrible sense of fashion. They often choose colors that look awful together. They don't mind if you suggest clothes that would make a nicer-looking outfit.

Dweebs are not very smart and they are a little bit clumsy. So you have to watch them closely. Things have a way of breaking with Dweebs around.

One day Sparky went into my room and saw a pretty orange dress he wanted to play with. It happened to be on one of my favorite dolls at the time. When he tried to get the dress off of the doll, her little plastic head broke off. Sparky didn't know what to do, so he ran around in circles with the doll's head in his mouth and his little wings flapping wildly. Boy, was I surprised.

Dweebs can't help being clumsy and breaking things. I always let Sparky know I still love him right away when he has an accident. Besides, it's hard to be angry with them because they are just so cute.

You can tell when a Dweeb is unhappy. It will make a clicking sound with its front teeth. When they are happy, they make a soft hooting sound.

Dweebs especially love board games. They can't actually play the games; they just like to be in the middle of the activity. Every time we start to play a game at the table, the little Dweebs, Flash and Gleep, jump right onto the board. They follow the playing pieces around, making little chirping sounds to each other after each move.

If anyone takes too long to make a move, the Dweebs start to fuss and chatter and hop up and down. They won't stop until the next playing piece is moved.

Once I caught little Gleep cheating. When no one was looking, she moved my father's playing piece ahead two spaces. But Flash saw her and made a big fuss, fluttering his wings and clicking loudly. He wouldn't stop until she finally turned red with embarrassment and gently slid the piece back where it belonged with her tail.

Many people think that all dragons can breath fire. This is not true. A few breeds of dragon will shoot out some sparks when they sneeze, and I have even seen one or two that blow out smoke rings when they burp. But I have only seen one dragon that actually was able to breathe fire, and he had help.

My brother Jeffery was feeding Sparky beans one afternoon. He noticed that when Sparky sneezed, a flame shot out of his mouth. This surprised Jeffery. It really surprised Sparky.

Two days later I learned that Jeffery had trained Sparky to make fire on command. He would feed Sparky a whole can of baked beans and then blow a pinch of pepper at him to make him sneeze. Whoosh! A flame would shoot from Sparky's mouth.

Always remember Dweebs are rather clumsy. If you have a Dweeb, watch it closely because it might accidentally start a fire. Especially if it has a cold.

Dragons love to play outside, especially Swifts. They are very fast runners. When they run, they spread their wings out, and after a few steps they hop up and glide for a foot or two. Sometimes they stumble a bit when they land, but they hardly ever fall. Swifts also love to climb up on wagons or bicycle seats, and then jump off so they can practice their landings.

Swifts hate to be alone. They like to run and play in groups. If you decide to have Swifts, you will need at least four or five.

Some dragons can fly. If you happen to have a Spot, for example, be sure to take it outside where there is plenty of room to swoop and zoom. Ashley and I even taught our Spots to jump rope. It was easy because Spots fly like hummingbirds, zipping through the air and then abruptly stopping to hover in place.

We named this kind of Dragon "Spot" because they are ashamed of their stripes. In fact, they are embarrassed by anything with stripes. They attack candy canes and become quite agitated when they happen to land on my lined notebook paper.

Spots are naturally curious. When they find something new, the first thing they do is pick it up, fly to the ceiling and then drop it to see if it bounces. They love things that bounce. Ping pong balls and tennis balls are good toys for Spots. Eggs are not.

Floaters can't really fly. They float by inflating themselves like a puffer fish. Their wings are really more like fins, which they use to guide themselves around in the air currents.

You will find that Floaters are very peaceful. Indoors they are happy to float around in your room for hours at a time humming softly to themselves.

Floaters also enjoy being outside, but it is important that you keep them on a leash. It is easy to make a leash from a piece of string. They are graceful and delicate, but they have little control outdoors, especially in a strong breeze. Watch them closely so they don't get caught in a tree or electrical wires.

Floaters love to travel, too. You can take them on trips with you in the car, and they will float along at the window looking at all the new sights along the way. When you travel with your Floater, don't forget to bring its leash so you can take it outside to explore.

If you already own a cat or dog, a Floater may be the perfect dragon for you. They simply float up and away from other pets that want to play rough. If you have pet birds, though, watch them around Floaters. Sometimes a bird will try to land on a Floater. A Floater can't carry much weight, so they both go tumbling. This embarrasses the Floater, and often it will try to hide in a potted plant all afternoon.

Floaters are very eager to please and love helping with minor chores. My Floater helps me with my housework by snagging the cobwebs from up near the ceiling.

The tail of a Floater is stretchy like rubber. I found that if I hold Puff by her front fins and stretch her tail out, then let it go, she snaps across the room like a rubber band. She bounces off the wall and tumbles through the air. You might think this would hurt but it doesn't. Puff loves this game and always comes right back, wriggling her tail toward my hand.

The Thumper is one of the largest dragons. They take up quite a bit of space, but they are very gentle and rarely break anything. They are named for the thumping sound they make with their tails.

Thumpers love music and will thump along softly, keeping perfect time. Their tails are hollow so they can make many different sounds, depending on which part they thump. They have very sensitive ears, so you must be careful not to play loud rock music or to raise your voice around them.

Thumpers like to swim in lakes and ponds. They are wonderful with children and can help them learn to swim. But don't take your Thumper in a swimming pool. The chemicals in the water are bad for their skin and sting their eyes.

A properly cared-for dragon will live for forty to sixty years. They can live even longer if you spend lots of time with them and let them know that you love them.

The Domo is known to live the longest of all dragons. Domos have been reported to live for 127 years as pets. Deciding to own a Domo is a lifelong commitment. In Japan the family Domo is given to the oldest child when he or she leaves home. This brings luck to the new household.

A Domo will always bow in greeting when someone enters the room. They also bow to say "thank you" and "goodbye." Warning: If you leave to go on vacation, make sure you return your Domo's bow, or when you come home you may find it right where you left it, still bent over.

This is by far the most intelligent kind of dragon. When properly trained a Domo can understand many words. They can be taught to write short messages on a computer or a typewriter, but they often have trouble spelling words correctly. Naturally, they tend to spell by the way words sound.

Domos communicate by making a humming sound. At times it almost sounds like they are talking. When several Domos are together they harmonize, making the most beautiful music.

Domos are fond of jigsaw puzzles. They will sit and work on one for hours at a time. They often put all of the edge pieces aside in a pile. Then they work the rest of the puzzle, saving the edge pieces for last.

They enjoy looking at comic books and playing video games, but they especially love watching television. Our Domo likes game shows the best. Whenever a contestant says the wrong answer, he gets agitated, flips his tail back and forth, and mumbles to himself in low tones.

He also seems to enjoy old Japanese monster movies. When the monster comes on the screen our little Domo laughs and rolls around the floor holding his sides. His other favorites are *National Geographic* specials about animals. He watches the clock, and when it's time for *National Geographic* to come on, he ties himself in a knot around my leg. I think he is waiting for the day they do a special on dragons.

Pet Dragons

COMMON NAME / LATIN NAME / FAVORITE FOOD

SPOT
Bouncimus Backus
Mexican Jumping Beans, Grasshoppers

FRED
Stealimus Sockus
Stinky Cheese, Sock Toes

SWIFT
Hurryum Upus
Fast Food, Flies, Fries

BARBRAD
Barbramus Bradimus
Broccoli, Beetles, Booger Biscuits

DOMO
Domo Arigato
Popcorn, Sushi, Alphabet Soup

NIDGET
Timerous Trembelus
Little, non-threatening round food like peas
and olives

THUMPER
Tympanius Legato
Beets, Dust Bunnies

DWEEB
Maximus Dweebus
Baked Beans, Burnt Marshmallows

CAMO
Gluetenous Frigidarium
Everything!

FLOATER
Excelsior Aerobis
Lite snacks, Spiders, Spaghetti

Melissa kept her agreement. She kept up her grades and took very good care of her dragon pets. At the end of the school year Uncle Fred told Melissa she could keep the dragons during the summer break. It was his busiest time of year, and he just didn't have room to keep them in his shop.

When summer break was over, Uncle Fred paid a visit to Melissa at her home. Melissa showed him the notebook she had been keeping and introduced him to the dragons. She showed Uncle Fred how each one was special in its own way. He saw how much Melissa had come to love her little friends and what good care she was taking of them. He couldn't bring himself to take them away from her.

Uncle Fred talked to Melissa's parents, and they all agreed that Melissa could keep the dragons if she wanted them. Needless to say, Melissa was a very happy little girl.

Uncle Fred fell in love with the little dragons, too. He made excuses to come and visit Melissa every week. They decided that if any of Melissa's dragons ever had their own babies, Uncle Fred could sell them in the pet store. In the meantime, he was often seen out in front of his shop looking up and down the street for a special delivery truck with an extra special cargo.

About the Authors

Ron and **Val Lindahn** live deep in the woods of the North Georgia mountains with their son Sean, two cats, a dog, two birds, an occasional opossum, several dragons and some very promising eggs.

Val has worked as an illustrator for 25 years, bringing magic and a sense of wonder to life through her paintings in books, magazines, posters and movies. In addition to creating award-winning images, Val is an accomplished sculptor, cook and gardener, and is an expert in hairball analysis.

Ron has spent the past 48 years wearing his inner child out. Along the way he has worked as a professional photographer, filmmaker, ski instructor, jeweler, graphic designer, writer, yoga teacher, marketing consultant, illustrator, nail banger and mechanic, and he plays bass guitar with the Atomic Fireballs.

Val and Ron are judges for the international L. Ron Hubbard Illustrators of the Future contest.